21 Ways To Use Social Media
by Maria Gudelis

With: Carlos "Art" Nevarez

"Steal" These Ways To Maximum Social Media Success!

How To Enjoy Using Social Media And Profit From It.

Editorial Director: Trish Gilliam
Cover Design: vMedio LLC
Production and Composition: vMedio Publishing

For information about special discounts for bulk purchases, please contact vMedio Publishing, a division of vMedio, LLC at (888) 747-6049 or <u>www.MariaGudelisHelp.com</u>.

More great published books by Maria Gudelis:

7 Step Action Plan to Getting Speaking Gigs
The Twitter Business Advantage

Table of Contents

Foreword by Craig Burton

Introduction

Foreword

by Craig Burton

I watched a YouTube video of an influential technology speaker on the topic of Social Media the other day. His presentation was powerful.. I don't remember much of what he said except his example.

"To prove to you my point of the relevancy of Social Media, let me give you a demonstration" he said.

I was skeptical that he could come up with something that would wow an audience in a simple demonstration.

"Give me a topic, any topic" was his request.

"Haiti" was quickly shouted from the audience.

Given the recent catastrophic events recently in Haiti, it sounded like a hot—and difficult—topic to me.

The speaker opened his browser to Google and typed in the search term "Haiti" so everyone could see.

Nine out of the ten results were about travel information and the Wikipedia entry on Wiki. Only one entry was about news and relief aid.

"Now watch what happens when I tap into Social Media" he pronounced.

The speaker then typed in a twitter search for "#Haiti."

My jaw dropped. Live, real-time conversations going on between people in Haiti and people doing things NOW to help.

It's not that Google isn't useful. It's just can't stand in the shadow real time social media.

That same instantaneous cause and effect that is happening in social media with world events is happening between people doing business. Social media is more than a trend, it is changing the way business works.

21 Ways to Use Social Media is just the tip of the iceberg. Get it, Get involved, Get social!

-Craig Burton

Craig Burton's contributions to computing have earned him recognition as one of the industry's most influential analysts www.CraigBurton.com/

Introduction

In this book, you are about to get 21 powerful ways to use Social Media that you can "steal" and implement into your own business right away to increase profit.

How to get more sales - Powerful Social Media tools that will help you attract new clients fast!

You want to know how to get more clients.

I understand how you feel. In fact, I used to be in that same jam. Working like crazy and not getting anywhere fast.

I was a wreck.

So I fully understand what you're going through. But I have a secret for you... and here it is:

I finally figured out how to get more clients and so can you. I just didn't know the secret strategies it took to get them. But once I finally discovered the right approach to getting more leads, things started to take off fast.

This is great news for you and me, especially since we want to know how to make our businesses grow quickly.

Now here's the cool thing. So many people haven't figured this out yet, which means we're ahead of the game. But we need to hurry because a lot of them will catch up -- sooner or later. Maybe sooner than you think.

Let's look at something...

When you start doing business with someone new. when you first buy something from them, or use their services...

What makes you decide to buy from them? Were they throwing brochures in your face? Were they cold calling you? Did you meet them at a networking meeting and they would just sell, sell, sell you?

Not likely!

I understand there are lots of people still doing that, but it just doesn't work.

So instead, let me tell you about a powerful client getting secret that does work...

Two words: Social Media

That's right! Here are just a few examples of social media that are very effective:

1) Twitter

Twitter is a fantastic lead generation tool, provided you use it correctly.

2) YouTube

YouTube is a powerful free tool that allows you to brand yourself and reach thousands of prospects fast.

3) Facebook

How would you like to reach a potential market of over 350 million users? If Facebook were a country, it would be bigger than the size of the United States of America! Facebook is one FREE social media site you simply cannot ignore.

It quite simply is 'not just for kids' anymore. In fact, two-thirds of comScore's U.S. Top 100 websites and half of comScore's Global Top 100 websites have implemented Facebook Connect, which literally can transform the way we interact on the web as it provides a two way conversation between consumers and your company.

Give them a chance to get to know you!

Warning: Don't be left out in the cold! If you want to know how to get more clients, you need to pay attention to this rule.

If this sounds intimidating, or you don't even know where to start, fear not. Check out my super cool marketing how-to video that lays out the whole system for you.

In less than 20 minutes, I'll show you exactly how you can build a relationship with your potential customers.

You can access the video here:
http://vMedio.com/marketingvideo

In this book, *21 Ways To Use Social Media*, I'll show you quick tips and tricks on how to benefit from the most active and free social media sites online today!

Way 1
Keep It Real!

One of the reasons why reality shows are so popular on TV right now is this:

IT IS WHAT THE MARKET WANTS!

What you want to do with any type of social media online is to be 'real'. You want to develop a Know-Like-Trust relationship. Where people can get to know, like and trust you. They don't want to know just about you in a stuffy suit in a business office.

For instance, they want to know if you love gourmet cooking, or if you love to travel. Do you love to run? Do you have any dogs? Things like that. Keep this in mind.

That is what this is all about!

Way 2
Join The Conversation!

Belonging to social media sites is like visiting a virtual water cooler. You need to join the conversation around other like-minded people.

Keep in mind your conversation should be 80% interest and 20% business.

Remember, if you are constantly all about business or all about buying your product, you will lose a lot of interest from other people and that is not 'keeping it real'.

Way 3
Have a Strategy in Place!

Those Who Don't Plan
Plan To Fail.

Let me tell you a story of two business owners I heard about from Jay Abraham.

The first one sent a mailing campaign and made about $2000 after about $7000 in expenses. That is it: $2000. To make more money he would have to repeat all that hard work over again.

The second business owner did a similar campaign, but he HAD A STRATEGY IN PLACE. He followed up with all the individuals who bought with a phenominal sales letter in the product that was sent to them. Because of the sales letter and the back-end strategy, he made $2,500,000 that year!

Which business owner do you want to be?

Way 4
Geo Target

What does that mean? Say you are a realtor, and you are selling real estate in a certain city, you can use a tool like **www.Twellow.com** to start following people on Twitter who live in your area or neighborhood.

This is a phenominal way to Geo-Target your market!

Isn't it great that you can create a community that is geographically oriented? Then when you are ready to deliver deals or coupons specific to that area you have a targeted following that you can use to make money with for your business!

Let me show you the power of geo-targeting.

Naked Pizza, a New Orleans restaurant, has done a successful geo-targeted campaign to create over 4300 followers who are in the surrounding area.

They used great 'offline' advertising, such as a big billboard above their restaurant saying:

"Follow Us For Specials"
www.Twitter.com/NakedPizza

Naked Pizza has attributed 20% of their annual one million in revenue to Twitter.

That equates to $200,000.

$200,000 divided by 4300 geo-targeted followers
(stats from July 2009)

Gives Naked Pizza a value per follower of:

Over forty dollars!

"If your business doesn't have anything to tweet about, you better shift into a business that does have something to tweet about!"

-Jeff Leach co-founder of Naked Pizza

Way 5
Drive Customers To Your Blog

It is very important to take advantage of all the traffic out there on the social media sites.

This is a very effective social media tactic as you now can start building your community around your blog. Which will allow you to brand your company or yourself even more by advertising special offers. You will need to include a lead capture or opt-in form to start building your list of interested prospects.

Include some kind of free report or call to action – get them to come back to your website or your blog. Otherwise, you are leaving a lot of money on the table!

Way 6
Turn Browsers Into Buyers

You are in business, right?

That's why you want to use social media for your business and for yourself. Not only do you want to brand yourself, but you want to get all the individuals, who are interested in what you have to say, into your sales funnel. That way you can turn browsers into buyers.

So how do you turn browsers into buyers?

You should use an automated lead capture system.

Wouldn't you want a 24-7 virtual employee working for your business? You can do that by using such marketing systems as Aweber, Constant Contact, or Get Response. This helps you stay conected with your prospects and customers.

You can have a marketing company help you implement this. Feel free to contact vMedio Inc. at (888) 747-6049 to help you market your company.

Way 7

Have a Strong, Sexy Call-To-Action!

Make sure you give out something very valuable for FREE, that will entice them to sign up to your list.

This is known as your "irresistible offer", making it simply irresistible for someone to sign up to get your free video, report, or special offer!

It is imperative to have this on your website, blog, or Facebook fan page to start building your list. It will mean the difference between getting one sale versus getting hundreds of sales.

If you are not great at writing ad copy, I suggest you hire an expert. You can also get great ideas by looking at popular magazines. Each headline of a magazine cover has excellent copywriting. You can use that for your own creative ideas!

Way 8
Have a Direct Response Marketing Campaign

Make sure you use some sort of automated email marketing system. This way you can capture all those leads and precious traffic that come to your site.

Then start a relationship with them.

Marketing statistics say that you need to touch a potential customer five to seven times before they buy from you and become a customer.

Wouldn't you want to do that in an automated way?

Way 9

Maximize Your
Twitter Profile!

When you set up your FREE Twitter account, you can have a custom graphic added as your background in Twitter.

That way whenever someone goes to your Twitter site, you can have a graphic that actually has that sexy Call-To-Action on it.

Make sure to include a picture of yourself in the top left corner.

Additionally, the text biography of your Twitter profile should include your targeted key words.

Way 10
Use Video, It Works!

We are in the reality society!

People want REALity!

Start by bringing people back to a video on your blog, or on your YOUtube channel.

Create a free Youtube channel branded for yourself, or use **www.viddler.com.**

Did you know that FORD modeling agency increased their sales in one year alone by over 140% just by using 'reality-style' videos on a FREE Youtube channel?!

Make sure to put the videos on your blog as well and be sure to ask for comments, so they can join the virtual water cooler conversation about your video!

Way 11
Hold a Contest

How about in one given month you hold a contest amongst all those who follow you on Twitter. Offer a Prize! Make it valuable - maybe even a $500 gift certificate!

Trust me, the amount of followers you get and the potential customers you get will be well worth that measly $500 investment!

Maybe you could go HUGE! Maybe you want to give away a FREE CAR! When you do that, you'll really get a lot of followers and that would be worth something for you!

One great example is how Universal Studios gets massive traffic and leads with 'activity contests' on their Facebook Fanpage.

(www.facebook.com/UniversalStudios)

Way 12
Increase Sales with Special Offers & Coupons

This is one of the most valuable ways to use Twitter, especially if you are a business owner or executive.

For example, did you know that computer maker, Dell, by offering Twitter-only discounts, generated $3,000,000 in sales? That is right - 3,000,000 in sales in just one year alone!

It is very powerful to start using coupons and discounts for just your Twitter business community.

What you need to do in order to become successful is come up with special offers available only for your Twitter followers.

Imagine the increase in sales you can have with just this alone! Think of the savings! Instead of printing coupons and spending lots of money to send them in direct mailers to homes, imagine how much money you could save with a 140-character line that is VIRTUAL and FREE!

Way 13
Engage New Customers with Surveys!

Using surveys in marketing for business in not a new tactic. However, with the advance of so many free social media sites, what you can do is direct traffic back to a survey.

The whole purpose of social media is to engage your potential customers and your existing customers into a conversation. The more feedback you get from them, the more you can service the desires and needs of your customers.

One free survey tool you can is online at **www.surveymonkey.com**.

Translation: More Sales!

Way 14
Create Buzz by Building Story Telling

Everyone wants to know a story. This is why reality shows are so popular right now. It is because people are engaged in the story, and the reality of what is happening. You can do that using social media. Your tweets, and what you say on Facebook can simply be a story. You can write about how you created your business for example.

For instance, one restaurant alone, before it even opened, started to tweet about the reasons why they were opening the business. The fun and even not-so-fun aspects of getting the restaurant opened. In doing this they actually built, within the community around the restaurant, a group of potential customers.

Come opening day, they already had a very active targeted group of people to come into the restaurant.

Way 15
Customer Service

Social media is transforming customer service. Now, you can have a two-way conversation. Never before has the power of "one" been networked with many other "ones" globally via social networking sites so that a business can interact one-to-one or one-to-many.

When a customer complains to you about your product, you can engage in a two-way conversation right away and fix the problem before he or she even has a chance to call your normal customer service number.

This gives you the chance to turn your customer into a loyal fan!

You can now have actual conversations with your customers and act on any customer questions and/or problems in 'real time' by monitoring the conversations around your brand.

You can monitor your name or brand by using Twitter Search at **http://search.twitter.com/** and simply enter your name and get the results.

You can also set your name or brand up in Google Alerts at **http://www.google.com/alerts** (note - you will need to set up a gmail account if you don't have one already,) and Google will send you the email results every day or how ever often you want!

Way 16
Build Your Brand With A Facebook Application

One of the "hidden" secrets to using Facebook to get more leads and increase your brand awareness is developing a Facebook application.

The path to success with developing a Facebook app is quite simply to market something that is fun, unique and at the same time, take advantage of lead generation and sponsorship through that community.

Think of it like having a hit TV show like 'Friends' and advertising revenues that were generated with the millions of viewers.

Even if you are a small business owner or entrepreneur, you could develop some sort of social type of game for Facebook with your brand on it.

One of the most lucrative apps on Facebook is Mob Wars with 2.5 Million active users (Source VentureBeat.com)

What is Mob Wars about?

In the game, a would-be mafioso starts off as a petty thief and must work his way to the top of the crime chain, earning points by fighting opposing gangsters, doing jobs, robbing stores and casinos and exploiting underlings. The player can improve his character by spending these points on better guns, real estate, loyalty and more, and while he could spend an eternity building up enough points to become a serious baller, he can also spend real cash to jumpstart the process.

Who says crime does not pay?

Way 17
Go Global

The image below alone illustrates the power of using Facebook as you see the number of users. This image was taken from www.InsideFacebook.com December 2009

Country	December	January	%	Change	Penetration
U.S.	98,105,020	102,681,240	5%	4,576,220	33.6%
Indonesia	13,870,120	15,301,280	10%	1,431,160	6.7%
Philippines	8,025,420	8,806,300	10%	780,880	9.7%
Turkey	16,327,880	16,961,140	4%	633,260	24%
Italy	12,993,120	13,500,300	4%	507,180	22.6%
India	5,174,200	5,658,080	9%	483,880	0.5%
Mexico	6,211,620	6,671,560	7%	459,940	6.3%
Spain	7,401,620	7,827,180	6%	425,560	17%
Malaysia	3,837,920	4,236,960	10%	399,040	15.3%
Argentina	7,187,360	7,526,920	5%	339,560	18.9%

Note: all of this data is based on estimates of monthly active users made available by Facebook through its advertising tool. It typically seems to be around one month behind Facebook's current stats; the company announced 350 million monthly actives back on December 1st, for example, and now we're seeing that number a month later.
Source: http://www.insidefacebook.com/

What company wouldn't want to be a part of a 350 million a month active user community?

Be ready to start getting international customers by using social media.

Way 18
Use Social Media for Social Good!

Social Media isn't just for profit! There have been some incredible success stories regarding raising money for a specific charity or local communities raising funds for local families in need.

There is one instance where my colleague's teenage nephew, while travelling in another country, was mugged and left injured, with no money in a foreign country.

Within hours of activating her global social network on Twitter and Facebook, individuals in that specific city were able to help and, more importantly, asssure to worried-sick parents and aunt that he was ok.

All you have to do is start with a 140-character sentence to reach out and ask for help!

Way 19

Raise $1,000,000 for Cancer?

One example of a social networking campaign for good, comedian Drew Carey announced that as soon as @DrewfromTV and @LiveStrong on Twitter combined hit one million followers, he would donate one million dollars to Livestrong.

$1 Million to Livestrong for 1 Million followers by end of '09. Read about it at CBS, who pay my salary. http://bit.ly /7F04J

1:24 PM Oct 7th from web

So go ahead and click on your follow button to follow **@DrewFromTV** and **@Livestrong** once you are logged into your Twitter account.

Way 20
Get onto Page One of Google!

One of the key benefits to being on Page one of Google or other top search engines is that you get more traffic.

Quite simply, more traffic translates to more sales for your business.

Search engines are sites, such as Google, where you enter a certain 'search term' and the software returns a list of website results based on those terms. For instance, if you typed in 'handmade cowboy boots', you'd see a list of websites show up on page one of Google that most likely are websites where you can buy cowboy boots.

You can see the benefit for any business to be on the first page of a top search engine.

Way 21

Explosive Use to Create Monetary Value of Your Social Media Assets

When you start creating social media sites for yourself or your company, you are creating assets that you can sell in the future!

Let's look at the blogging explosion we've seen over the last few years. The movie "Julie and Julia" opened the world's eyes about the power of blogging. It took blogging main-stream for many who had no idea that an average person could get attention, socialize with the world and pursue their passion using a simple blogging platform available to the masses for free.

Let's take a look at just some successful 'Blog It and Sell It" stories: The Bankaholic blog was sold for $15 million. ArsTechnica sold for $25 million. PaidContent sold for $30 million.

One doctor phoned his competitor and offered $10,000 for his newly created blog and social media assets!

We will see, in this new decade, individuals and corporations starting to value their social media assets as a true 'physical' asset, and you should start your own social media portfolio now to take advantage of this huge wave of opportunity!

My Bold Prediction:

In fact, I wouldn't be suprised if you start hearing investment analysts discussing a company's "social media asset value" as an indicator whether an investor should buy or sell a company's stock!

I hope you enjoyed this book, *21 Ways to Use Social Media*, and if you'd like to find out how my marketing company can help you with your social media asset portfolio creation, please call us at 888-747-6049 or drop me an email at Maria@vMedio.com.

Free Social Media Tips

Free CD offer

Let me send you my CD "Simple Social Media Trends to Boost the Earning Power of Your Business."

All you need to do is get online and go to:

www.vMedio.com/freecd

to get it rushed to your door!

29

But What's Next?

Here's Something Else:

You get a FREE Social Media Profit
Analysis (value over $495!)

Here's how to get it;

Please contact our office
at 888-747-6049 and
give us the special word
"profits".

Appendix

Facebook Statistics right from the 'Facebook Pressroom'

The following data was taken as of January 2010 from Facebook's website.
If you wish to get the latest statistics, please visit the page:

http://www.facebook.com/press/info.php?statistics

More than 350 million active users

50% of our active users log onto Facebook in any given day

More than 35 million users update their status each day

More than 55 million status updates posted each day

More than 2.5 billion photos uploaded to the site each month

More than 3.5 billion pieces of content (web links, news stories, blog posts, notes, photo albums, etc.) shared each week

More than 3.5 million events created each month

More than 1.6 million active Pages on Facebook

www.ingramcontent.com/pod-product-compliance
Lightning Source LLC
Chambersburg PA
CBHW041146050326
40689CB00001B/510